THE GREEN MONK

When I read a Marcus Slease poem I am reminded that the world is made up of billions of parts, each with their own soul, each with a great ability to illuminate the sacred while also misbehaving. Slease is a poet that reminds us the wildness of life is not something we can control or even fight against but rather something we should witness and honour.

— Matthew Dickman, Author of *Wonderland*

THE GREEN MONK

MARCUS SLEASE

BOILER HOUSE PRESS

BUILT TO SPILL

PSYCHIC MARMALADE

THE GREEN MONK

GREAT EXPECTATIONS

To travel! To change countries! / to be forever someone else... / the absence of any goal / And any desire to achieve it!
— Fernando Pessoa

Everybody has a geography that can be used for change that is why we travel to far off places. Whether we know it or not we need to renew ourselves in territories that are fresh and wild. We need to come home through the body of alien lands.
— Joan Halifax

Dreams are severed fruit / Auburn pears have fallen in the field / Parsley blooms in the field / Sometimes the leghorn appears to have six toes / I crack an egg and the moon comes out.
— Chika Sagawa

After that first home, the second seems drafty and a hybrid.
— Rainer Maria Rilke

I've often lost myself, in order to find the burn that keeps everything awake.
— Federico García Lorca

The task of the right eye is to peer into the telescope, while the left eye peers into the microscope.
— Leonora Carrington

BUILT TO SPILL

BURNING GIRAFFE

after Salvador Dalí's painting Burning Giraffe, *1937*

Flowers devour a man. It floats and sinks. Floats and sinks. A river of red runs through it. Close your eyes. Are you only dreaming. Houseflies and horseflies hang on joints of meat teaching their young to fly. The windows sweat and sweat. Hard rain on the outside. Warm air on the inside. When you ain't got no flowers, you got the blues. When you ain't got no flowers, you got the blues. When you ain't got no flowers, you got the blues. When you ain't got no flowers, you got the blues. A burning giraffe in the distance. Sprinkle it with dew and a miracle or two. Wrap it in a sigh. Soak it in the sun. It sinks and floats. Sinks and floats. It is eternal flame and sunshine thru the rain.

My pillow takes on a creamy surface. Like a swan. Swans are sensual creatures. Soft swans. Velvet swans. A swan comforter to snuggle into for cold winters. Some folks rub the ribs. Some folks rub the glass. The blades around the shoulder. Some folks rub out. Some folks rub in. Some folks rub down and up. Some folks rub up and down. Some folks rub around. I rub my swan.

Hair greasy. Rather itchy. The boiler broken. No hot water. 4 days no shower. Musty wet wood for always musty apartment. This small cave saps energy. Sitting on bench on the Avenue of the Americas to warm my body. Ants on the march on dusty road. Roaring sun. So many ant civilizations. Men in orange vests trim the branches. Wave of motorcars. Buzz of motorcycles. Rivers and mountains without end. The fat demon on the television is an animation. The best thing to kum out uv englund iz fairee.

There are audible clouds blowing through the graveyard. Witches and brews and satchels of dream music. Dirges of hooves and the warm flanks of night. There are goings and comings. Flickerings and becomings. There are hugs and funions and giant sponges that soak in the sounds of the jungles. We have traveled so far and also nowhere. There are stained sheets and clean sheets blowing and blowing against the mouth of the cave.

Night comes and they re-enter the land of mustard. There is a mustard wheel. You can ride the mustard wheel in a glass cage to get a bird's eye view of the financial capital. There is fancy mustard straight from the heavens. There is ancient mustard straight from the earth. There is artificially enhanced mustard. Skeleton trees and smog holes. Smudged hoof prints in the sand.

ANCIENT ELEPHANTS

after Salvador Dali's Painting One Second Before the Awakening from a Dream Provoked by the Flight of a Bee Around a Pomegranate, *1944*

A misty rain. Swelling slugs. A buzzing out the window. First there is one bee. Then a hundred. Then thousands. So many bees. There is a pomegranate on the ground and the bees are buzzing around it. A fish sprouts from the pomegranate. Then a tiger sprouts from the fish. Then another tiger sprouts from that tiger. Pretty soon I am going to die. The bees stop buzzing. A tall woman with closed eyes leans on a hazel stick. She points to the sky. This is your elephant she says. It is an ancient elephant. It walks on giant stilts. I am too low. It is too high. I will have to watch it go by.

In the midst of wrestling with the demons, he suddenly finds herself being groomed — thrusting him into increasingly dangerous measures. Blood sugar sex magik plays on the hi-fi. He washes the dishes in the miniature sink. The shoe holder is a smudge holder. The sludge of time smudges all the corners. He sweeps the floor of toenails and skin dust. Everything beneath the feet is water. He scrubs the cakey toilet and wipes the windows. The small square is full of people blinking into the bright sun. The small square is full of electric hums. The people crowd into them on the way to nowhere. I doubt therefore I am he says. I ejaculate into the void he says. In heaven the most open vagina closes its doors. In heaven the most bulbous ball sacks swing from the sky like chandeliers. Destruction and creation. These are the days of our lives he says. Almond blossom confetti. Sideways walking ants. Ripples on the line.

RUSTY

The yellow subtitles under the demon says what did he do with it. What did he do with it. My time is rusty. Descend slowly. I have pierced the last hole in my belt. My grandfather collected milk from the farmers. I read all the *Farmer's Weekly*. Short term memory to long term memory requires contemplation and reflection. Matter is energy slowed down. Hold the handle of the mop. Glide the mop in slow gentle motions. Your hands should embody effortless effort. Where am I in this equation.

GHOSTLY TURNIP GREEN GLOW

Born in Northern Ireland of French Huguenot Silcock stock. We have spotted the rabbit ears. We have spotted a ghostly green turnip to turn away crows. At day's end: hollow mountain. Black sails. Silver trees. Dark thickets and thick crickets. A reservoir of music heavy and light in the throat.

My grandfather clipped hedges in Northern Ireland. My great grandfather was a gardener for rich Anglo Irish. My mother is a cleaner. My step father fixes air conditioners. My biological father was a gardener in Belfast. They cut off one of his toes. I have a bad toe. I have a bad knee. I am tracing my ancestry. I like the ground. I come from the ground. The earth peoples like an apple tree apples sez Alan Watts. It's 5.23. Sirens are going off. I ride the underground. I come from working class roots. Who doesn't? I do not know how to hammer. When I worked construction I could not find the stud. I am not a man. I am not a woman. I am riding the underground. Where does it go? Nobody knows.

In the morning fog the dead milkmen clink their milk bottles. Rattlesnakes sun themselves on the footpath. Turning 43 in one week. What is the magic. The bones popping & creaking. My old face carved into the tree. I take the stone steps to the underground. The milky moon creams the waters. When you wake up you hit rock bottom. No rock. No bottom. Bone crystals in the skull chain. Dragon rocks of dream.

Eyes sucked through a straw. Left eye twitch. Right eye twitch. The big toe breaks through the shoe. There is a key beneath the knee. Rub it gently. Heads of hair out the window. The cars sputter and choke. The coal burning tickles the throat. A giant egg on the table. It squeaks in the boiling water. Fire on the mountain.

The animals know their way home. A constant void and profound mystery soaks their layers. Crawling under bushes. Burrowing under rocks. An ancient hiss & armor. The forked eyes of the tongue. They hoot & dream dervish. They crawl up the walls to soak in the sun.

An alien rumble shook the windows. The snow ashed. The green marbles guttered. The curbs crumbled. The living room was another planet. The hands piled on top of his head. They whispered for the holy ghost. The dark honey of the forest dripped onto his tongue. His neck bobbed. His ear drums full of water. An alien dragonfly buzzed his ear. The pecans dropped from the pecan trees. The peaches dropped from the peach trees. The worms wormed. The alien had a glowing red finger. He looked at his finger. It was not glowing. He did not call home.

Walking to work in goon suits. The drains burp and gurgle. Roaming the rolling hills of sewage and dung balls. The hidden musty pipes snake the city. Cockroaches smudge the walls. The dead refrigerator has stopped its deep hum. The dead refrigerator is musty. The smell of ripe melons is musty. Wet bathing suit filled with sand in the crotch is musty. The sardine train is musty. The smell of dust from the mountains. Musty. The earth tugs the earthworms. The earth tugs the sky birds. Bare branches scratch the moon ink.

ALMOST A STILL LIFE

The wild sheep rumble the ice chest. The wine barrels in the belly. The throat is full of shavings. Tuna. Red sauce. & flaking pastry. Bird and shadow. Apple and pineapple. The moon is full of worms. A wooden bird cracks its wings.

WOODEN OWL

Walking around the ring that rings the old town. The burden of brightness. Meaningless memorials. Green man blinking wait/walk wait/walk wait/walk. At day's end hollow mountain. Wooden owl.

The wind from outer space gnaws at our faces. It is hard to look over your shoulder. Sampled the amnesia. A trot down to Don Fruta for eggs and veggies. The wind flattens the grass. Memorials of midnight flowers. A deep blue purple cosmos. I will warm my frozen hands in the shower.

MILK OF THE POPPY

for Leonora Carrington

Pins and needles in the hand. Neck stiff. Back stiff. Knee stiff. It is time for the magic. The cauldron of my belly bubbles. 65th birthday beers with Larry. Plato's cave is moving inwards to crush us. Time is on the line. Memories in the haystack. What do we do with the shadows. The horned goat is holding a broom. The robed figures are preparing the food. The animal soul has another body. People and bisons on the horizon. We are feeling animals mostly.

Wasted limbs get smaller. Do they bury you for free if you don't cut the mustard. I brand myself on Instagram Twitter Facebook & Tumblr. The pop ups ding on the phone. Double dutching the cracks in the footpath. Drawing a line in the room to cross over. I blow up my buttocks with bar dips. I stuff my crotch with three socks. I frost my fringe with sun in. Riding the trains to warm my body. Rubbing my hands for an invisible future. The mold spreads from the sweaty windows and flakes the plaster.

PSYCHIC MARMALADE

SWOOP

They landed in Vegas with a little blue parachute. A retro heart space of one armed bandits and smoky red carpets. Buffet lines. Dust devils. German edelweiss hidden in bibles. The high school full of metal detectors and snipers. They drank rye whiskey in parked cars and slept in the rolling green parks of the homeless. Little blue drinks from the dews of the mountains. Little blue eyeshadow and short stockings. The lovely weather inside the skullhouse welcomed them for breakfast.

At the top of the street a crack house. At the bottom of the street a crack house. Around the corner a crack house. Outside scraps for air conditioners. Inside screaming children. Father wanted chickens. There is no room for chickens said mother. Father wanted a horse. There is no room for a horse said mother. Woody woodpecker with chocolate donuts for breakfast. A cracker with jam for lunch. On Sundays sweet pickles. Liver and onions. Bubble and squeak. Champed potatoes. At the top of street a school bus stuffed with itchy jumpers. At the bottom of the street tinted windows. Barred windows. Cracked windows. At the dusty park a jungle jim with monkey bars. See-saws. Gold chains and French kissing.

Where is my honor? It is a popped cherry. I swim in the cream. I backseat mambo. I bake the cookies. I boink and bonk and boom boom. I bunny hop and stump jump. I bone dance. I butter the muffin and buzz the brillo. I eat the cream puff in the enchanted forest in a four legged frolic. It is bed boogie. It is carnal gymnastics. Horizontal hula. Horizontal hustle. Hippity dippity. Jiggle juice & jump. Glazing the donut. Makin grass sandwiches. Makin bacon. Parking the pink plymouth in the garage of love. Play pickle-me, tickle-me. Play the game of twenty toes. Play tiddlywinks. Percy in the playpen. The bee in the hive. A bit of curly greens. A bit of giblet. A split mutton. A sugar stick. A summer cabbage. A nooner. Star gazing on your back. Throw a leg over. Throw another log on the fire. A squeeze and squirt. Walk the dog. Wallpaper the closet. Wind up your clock. Wink wink, nudge nudge. Work the hairy oracle. Yodeling in the valley. Yodeling in the gulley. Zallywhacking. Ziggy-wiggling. Zoinkering. Zwooshing the swoosh. Shake the sheets and shoot the moon. The candle in the pumpkin.

HORSE JAM

The shoes dangle from telephone wires. We have traveled from the dusty red rocks of Utah over the mountains and around the geysers. The thick paint of locusts & butterflies coat the windshield. The sign says beware of snakes. The grass thick and uncut. The muddy river a sludge of slow time. The coke machine a hollow hum. The sign says rest stop. The hammock hangs between trees. It is covered in fleas.

THE POTATOES OF PROMISE

All day cold feet. End to end. Under a blanket. We have sealed the ark with metal shutters. The bowels grumble in the belly. This last winter dreams more scarce. My friend the bladder the bagpipe the unearthly whisper. The potatoes of promise mature in dark wombs.

FOIL DINNER

In ghost town. Sitting on red rocks. Fingering the flint. Fingering the foil. The potato cooks in the ashes.

Chinese stars in my sleeve. Nunchucks in my backpack. I want to shoot fire from my fingers and become invisible. In America they show me hot dogs. Good hot dogs turn the bun pink. In American they show me baseball. The ball slaps the leather. I like the sound but not the action. In America they show me trucks. Old trucks are curvier than new trucks. Five-Alive in mother's basement. Plastic gold sunglasses for the sun. I am a warrior of light.

DARK GRASSES

After death your heart and a feather balance on a scale. There is nothing to fear. What did you do with the gift of human existence. The rubbish bins overflow with butts and beer bottles. The wooden railing overflows with plastic white roses. This is the beauty of earth. Burning white sea shells. Sun face of dark grasses. A purple glow.

SENTIENT SUN

for Rupert Sheldrake

The sun holds the planets in orbit. The sun bathes celestial bodies in energy. It grows the plants for earthlife. Plants make oxygen for us. There is a membrane around the solar system surrounded by helium pores. It's brain more complex than the electromagnetic patterns of human brains. Matter conscious. Electrons and atoms conscious. Stars conscious. Galaxies conscious. Sun conscious. The sun sends the solar winds. It decides when to send to it. The sun could send solar flares. It could shut down all human civilization. It is creation and destruction. The sun is concerned with its peer group. The other stars.

I keep adjusting the tongue of my shoe. The tongue of my shoe sez Camper. To camp among the stars with a little tent in the wilderness. The dead light of the heavens with no gods of goblins for pleasure. The liquid in my body turns to glass then shatters inside. A packet of chocolate buttons in my pocket. Lodestone versus touchstone. Pebbles transmigrate under the soles of my shoes. Shredded wheat floats in milk but the sugar sinks to the bottom.

Honey swirled into porridge. Psychic marmalade. The ancient power of fright and lust. Death and life embrace. The queen bee. Under the grassy hill. A seat of feathers. A seat of horsehair. The people of the goddess shape shift.

Small mouth. Ears large, bat-like, and erect. A bird of prey. Dzien Dobry. The compass spins. Sails puff out. Claws reach out to grab me. The hole is open. I clack my suitcase down the cracked streets. The green fairies skid off the roads and onto the walls. The trees ruffle their sleeves. The coal smogs the highways and byways. A blanket of blur surrounds me.

CIRCLES

“We kept going around in circles.” “We kept going around in the circles.” No “the” he says. “In Ikea we walked in the circles.” No “the” he says. “In Ikea we walked in circles.” “It felt like I was going around in circles” is not the same as “going around in circles.” When you are in Ikea “it feels like you are going around in circles”. “We kept going around in circles.”

OLD SHOES WITH GOOD TIMES IN THEM

A stunned German cockroach glides across my desk. A fly rubs its body on the window. The black mold is climbing the walls. Buns and bones in wooden shack. The hacking coughs of winter bang against the shutters. A shaded cave. Bells of a distant watch. Warm baton of bread in the park. Big blue sky before me. Nothing more to wish for. My white teeth are numbered.

A meeting center with metal stalls for horses. In the center of the circle little windows with the faces of old ladies. I approach the little window. 5zl she says. What is it I ask. Zapiekanka she says. What's zapiekanka I ask. It is sort of pizza she says. I give her the change in my pocket. I am very much in the mood for pizza. The pizza is very crispy. It is French bread pizza. Thank you I say. The mushrooms are from deep forest she says. Thank you I say. The mushrooms slip down my throat. Very good she says. I am overstuffed with pickled mushroom French bread pizza. The window with the old lady is becoming more and more steamy. There are so many zapiekanki in the oven. She curls her finger for me to come closer. I lean into the small window. The wiry hair of the old lady scratches my ear as she leans into me. The feast day is fast approaching she says.

LUXURY SALTS

I enter the toilet. You cannot see the sky. It is full of smog. A small package on the bathtub. Luxury salts. I fill the bathtub and dump the luxury salts. The water turns purple. Bubbles foam. I dip my feet in the water. It is warm and cozy. I slide down into the half claw tub and brush my face with the bubbles. I rub the bubbles all over my body. My skin becomes soft and supple. I rub my hands on my feet. It is soft and supple. I rub my ears and my eyes and knees. Traces of people fade into distant sky.

ALCHEMIA

for Leonora Carrington

The room sways with waves of music. Mushrooms on floral walls. Everything wooden and smoky. A greenish liquid is placed in front of me. It is green fairy. I drink one green fairy. And then another and another. I do not know how many. There is a rabbit hat. Bristling moustaches. Metallic noses. Various glitters and mud paints. The steps are wooden and weathered by many feet. At the bottom of the stairs there is a large room. It is mostly dark. Someone is plucking feathers from their neckline. Someone is flowering the skeletons.

COMMUNION

Shadows on the ceiling in the shape of birds with large swollen beaks. Angels with small golden trumpets. Their bodies slap together then peel away. Slap together and peel away.

FIRST STAR

Clubbing the carp in the bathtub. Boiling the juice of beetroot. Bubbling the cabbage in bacon. Creaming the mushrooms. Stewing the fruit in their juices. An extra plate for an invisible guest. Everyone is waiting for the first star.

SNOW GLOBE

Everyday I burn the porridge and bring it back to life. I take a picture out the window. It doesn't stick. The doorway hung with cobwebs. The chi of newborn softness. Ten thousand gateways. Ten thousand doorways. There are one million snowflakes and each one is different.

TRINKETS

The centre of the earth a giant magnet. What is the way to Cold Mountain. I have to learn to tap the phone with both thumbs. I am below average. A fiery sunset in the park. The aging tombs big and small. A planet populated with trinkets. The dusty world of empty dreams. A hill of pines hums in the wind.

The silent star. The silent sharks. The silent pebbles in the distance. The floating heart exquisite mystery. A transparent and ghostly seagull walks the railings. It hops along the footpath. She feels the sympathy of fish. And flowering trees. Time is short. Time is long. The bloated moon rubs its belly.

PALMS

The palm of the hand and the palm of the mind. The palms of Lorca. The palms of Jiménez. Madrid is full of palms. Outside the window is palm. Crocodile utopias and juicy oranges. Shepherd sticks in the valley that echoes with doubt. Wind in a box. Silver purified in a crucible. Gold refined seven times. These do not equal the power of palms. Break the palms. Flee like a bird to the palms. Rejoice in the palms. A shade for the weary and a home for the hairy spider. Everyone enjoy the palms.

SPRING FEVER

My friend my breast bones crack. My neck creaks. A living skeleton. And more. Mahou red beer on bird shit benches. Fingers cold. Stomach sour. Every morning of the world. Resurrection or rolling rock forever.

Roman water gods and the driftwood and to hike over islands to visit marketplaces and the food and the people. The great ships come and go. The sky on fire. Cobbled & crowned. Alone & happy. Walking by the surf & make fire in darkness. In the wild grass I am Ver Sacrum. I am sacred spring. Everyone. No one. Blowing Bubbles. Everyone. No one. Throwing babies in the air. In crunch position. Shaking hands with danger.

THE GREEN MONK

FIG LEAVES

We come in peace, they said. Welcome to the revolution. Some people had gathered in the medieval square. Others were hiding behind their red curtains in cold brick houses. He stepped forward & crawled around on the grass. A soft and silky blanket. Euphoria, he said. A woman stepped forward. She slicked back her hair while doing a snake dance. The aliens are coming she said. Suddenly they were all naked. They were a naked colony. Where are the fig leaves he said. There are no fig leaves she said.

He frosts the cracks. On his knees. Under the sink. Along the floor. On his tiptoes. Near the ceiling. Around the hinges. It is very smooth. Then it dries. He frosts more cracks. Around the kitchen sink. Around the fridge. Around the washing machine & cooker. Shadows flicker across the floor. They wiggle their radio antennas. Some find a special seat for a feast. They dip under the toilet seat to eat. He opens the refrigerator and twists the packages and clips them. He opens the cupboards and twists the packages and clips them. He sits at the wobbly table and looks at the three cacti. Tiny objects fly from the cacti. He claps his hands. He claps his hands. They fly through the cracks in his hands. The cracks grow. He frosts more cracks. The cracks grow. He frosts more cracks. The cracks grow. He frosts more cracks.

He went to the kitchen. The drain was blocked for the 223rd time. Onions and yellow curry. She rinsed them with fairy. You only need a small squeeze for a whole pile of dishes. Do not waste the fairy he said. There is plenty of fairy she said. The fairy is almost gone he said. It is only half gone she said. There are only a few squeezes left he said. There are many squeezes left she said. I want to waste the fairy she said.

TIGHT SQUEEZE

Dead fish on ice. At the neck of the lobster a giant soap bubble. She points to the flat fish. He scrapes the scales & points to the head. No she says. Sin cabeza. He deposits the head in the rubbish. There are many heads. It is a tight squeeze. He wraps the fish in plastic. And then more plastic. It is a tight squeeze. She heads to the counter. It is rush hour. No one has on their turn signals. It is a tight squeeze. She places the fish in the tiny oven. It is a tight squeeze. She moves sideways through the kitchen. It is a Spanish kitchen. There is only supposed to be one person in the kitchen. That one person is supposed to be very small. She is not small enough. It is a tight squeeze.

Up ahead there is a large group of middle aged Peruvian women. There is a laugh & also a scream. Another kind of ha ha. A laugh to chase away fear. Suddenly she sees it. A giant rat. More like a small cat. The rat stares at her. Then it runs past her. It does not stop to look back. She wets her whistle & dons her coat of many colours. Up the mountain a portal for small children. The hollowed cavern. Cabbage heads and sunken tea leaves. New nuts on old branches.

SWEATBOX

A long thin human is smoking a long thin cigarette. They think about thin. Thin mints. Thin trousers. Ghost thin humans smoking ghost thin cigarettes. Do they want to feel thin? And also thinner? They buy long thin white cigarettes and feel thinner. They disappear very quickly. One day they wake up craving a thick. Plugged with a yellow cork. Where does it come from? They smoke five thicks. They think about thin. They walk the dark tunnels toward the sweatboxes.

They follow the sun. They buy oranges and other sundry fruit. They drink a beer at local beer bars. They visit Desperados. Hola they say in a perky pitch. Meat from the stones por favor. Mole enchiladas por favor. The poacher's gun sits on the window. Out of the holes crickets and waterfalls. Out of the holes transparent tombstones. The sad train sits in the rain. The fog dresses the train. The further you go the longer the shadows grow. Hola they say in a perky pitch. Hola they say. Hola they say they say. Fish eggs and shots of vodka. Frog minnows and musty chickens. Rolling dreams in stockings. They walk the streets with little sticks in their teeth. They walk the streets with little sticks in their teeth. The diamond blaze of midnight. Bald babies stray dogs and shining scales. A river slides under the bridge.

At La Elipa park Latino music and crowds of children. Various small flyers in celebration of spring. They move their bodies to pop songs. Punching down and left and right and waving their hips. The spores of spring have sprung their strategies. It is very windy. The bees stick to themselves. The wasps warlike. The ants join together to carry debris to their nests. The phone vibrates my pocket. What is the reply. The reply is 45 minutes for happy hour. What about the laundry. Google says 1 day before rot and mildew. Energy level increase with curious open people is the best validation for art and existence.

TOMORROWLAND

for Méret Oppenheim

They turn on the drone. He places his clean shirt and jeans on the chair. Next to his side of the bed. The skin of the sky cracks open. An egg. He taps it against the sweating walls and puts it in their two sided fryer. He boils the bald egg in hot water. He looks out the steamy window. Bald heads of bread peep out of fur. A small tribe roast chickens over a fire. The bubbles are getting louder. It is very steamy. He pulls the eggs out of the boiling water. He opens the cupboard. The egg cups are coated in fur.

The rain finally came. It had been three months of no rain and lots of large beetles. When the rain came it was wet. It soaked the rooftops at the church outside the window. The holy choirs say ahhhh. After three months of blue skies and sun and beer gardens the rain came. Look out the window. It is wet. The birds show up. The holy birds say ahhhh. You can see the birds more. They flitter. And also the trees. The trees are greener against the gray sky. There are many filters. And also textures. Meditative, self-reliant, funny, alarming, strange, difficult, intelligent, and beautifully crafted. Also astonish, dismay, delight, confuse, tickle and generally improve the quality of our lives. The tender sounds of the rain in the trees from the heavens to the grounds and the grounds to the heavens. Rinse and repeat.

BAPTISM

She walks to the sink with her little clay pot and a satchel of salt. The satchel of salt is free of iodine. It comes from the deep mountains of the north. First she warms the water then she pours it into the clay teapot. She tears the satchel with her sharp canines and pours the pure contents into the little clay tea pot. Then she tilts her head to the left and pours the little teapot down her right nostril. All of the gunk comes out of her left nostril. She tilts her head to the right and pours the little teapot down her left nostril. All of the gunk comes out of her right nostril. Baptism is the key to everything. We baptise the dishes in soapy water so they can be used again tomorrow. We baptise the peaches pears and plums. We baptise our faces to wake up.

BRIGHT EYES

for Aaron Slease

His brother slept with Roland Rat. Roland Rat had floppy ears, a large pink tongue, and sometimes sunglasses. He slept with giant rabbits. One of the rabbits was called thumper. When thumper thumped his tail on the ground something was coming. Like big diggers. The big diggers ripped up the earth. They destroyed the bunkers. The red eyes of the rabbits glowed and glowed. They were called bright eyes burning like fire.

Young boys and girls are swapping the cards of saints. We do not have saints. We only have fish. We pull out our fish cards. We play Go Fish. Here is the game of Go Fish. I ask my partner for the face value. Alice I say. Do you have such and such face value. No says Alice. Go fish says Alice. I dive into the pool. I keep pulling and pulling. In this city fish is very popular. It is one of many fish centers. Neot is the patron saint of fish. He is only four feet tall. He is very small. In a book about St. Neot King Alfred burns the cakes. Why did he burn the cakes? He was supposed to be watching the cakes. The peasant woman scolds him. Watch the cakes Alfred says the peasant woman. But Alfred is worried about the barbarians. It is hard to watch the cakes when you are worried about the barbarians. The barbarians are just around the corner. They are always around the corner. We keep watching the cakes.

He rode in a maluch and dated a miner's daughter. The maluch was very small. They had to jump start it in winter. In summer it was rock climbing. The rock climbers pointed their toes into holes and angled their fingers. The rocks were rated. 6 and above meant very hard. The easier rocks looked like cheese. He was not good at jamming his fingers and toes into cramped spaces. He was not a good rock climber. He took pictures. He was a voyeur. Maybe also a voyager. At midnight Wisniowka from the bathtub. At dawn a silent kiss. It was Forever Young. It was 99 red balloons. The mirror on the sliding door was endless copulations. It was reality contaminated by dreams.

MESH

They put the bottom half of his body to sleep and kept the top half awake. This is new mesh from India they said. Top of the line they said. He could feel the pull. The tugs and stretches. He saw the little headlights from the doctors as they peered into his groin. It was reflected in the mirror above his head. He lay in bed with the drippings. Boli the nurse said. Boli he said. More drippings. He floated in the distance. The glass castle of other lives. Moon liquor in mayo jars. Moon moats and moon pies. The dogs yelped in the forest. Birds flapped in the trees. The catch of the day flapped in the nets. Silverfish tunneled through the grains.

Flamenco fans, beer huggers, small rubber squeegees to wipe the mirrors. They rub the lamp. There is no magic genie. There is no magic carpet. A salted cod climbs inside their mouth holes. They walk past the bull ring. It is a safe day for the bull ring she says. They enter the ring. The tables groan with vegetables. Barrels of salty pickles and wheelbarrows of watermelons. Giant Spuds covered in mud. Sprightly spring onions with their roots trailing behind them. They pick up the spud. It is shapely and very comely. It is a beautiful spud he says. They finger the spud and also the sprightly spring onions. It is a beautiful onion she says. They leave the bullring with their suitcases full of veggies. The wheels brake. They drag the suitcases on the ground. It is midnight. A lady's voice calls out the numbers. The numbers echo off the toothy buildings. They bounce off the washing line and metal shutters. They do not know if she is selling something or if it is a warning. They keep starting over. They leave one country for another.

GREEN MONK

The little green man beeps to walk across the street. The green monk imitates it. It has tiny ear tunnels and speaks many dialects. If you part the lighter feathers below the eyeholes and climb inside the ear holes what would you hear. Green. I want you green. The green monk is communal. Their nest contains multiple apartments. There are many entrances and exits. Everyone gets their own door. Some of the nests are as big as a whole car. Green. I want you green. I drink you green at daybreak. At nightbreak. At all moments between. The park benches sit in the sand beside the city's largest cemetery. It has a green entrance. The apartment blocks are toothaches. There are many metal shutters. At the top the green terrace is wooden. It is high above the roar of human traffic. Green. I want you green. Green rumbles. Thirsty green oozes. A green blanket. A green hairnet. The green tree rubs its back against the windows. The green stars of your neck bones. I want you green. Green wind. Green branches. Green trances of the green soil. Green honeysuckle on green hedges. Green sea foam of fine lace. Green. I drink you green. At morning. At daybreak. At all moments between. Green hills of wild strawberries. Green urn of wild ashes. Green milk of dawn time and noon time. We drink and we drink. Green. I want you green. The green monk travels many distances. The bristle of green feathers of the green monk. The long green hair of the wind.

GREAT EXPECTATIONS

They take the train up the mountain. The air conditioner is broken. It is the middle of winter. When they step off the train it is summer. They are shotgunned on the beach by a bubble maker. The World Cup is a great defeat. The fish bones are small and tender. The lemon soaks the skin. The horses run the gamet. The shower is a small cabin. The apricot tea. The prickly palms. The blue bouncy ball with two handles. The beer bubbles in the belly. The ants bob in the jelly. The mosquitos knit together. Yolk yellow sun sizzles on water. Night washes the shores of day.

To compensate for lack of blue on the island she paints the curtains sky blue. And also the walls. She lines up the glass bottles in the windows. Dead moths. Toast crumbs. The blender blends the carrots. The blender blends the shady nook and potatoes. The kitchen is full of pig's ears. Their white hairs bristle in the sizzling skillet. They walk to the market to finger the meats. Damp conversations spill from the pubs. Empty rubbish bags cling to their feet. Empty steam steams the air. From time to time they peep into the little window. The dough is rising. The stars are mutilated at nightfall. The cold rocks are warmed by the belly and sometimes the thighs. The meat is caking. The horse gallops down the hill. It is a good omen. The egg cracks on the table. It is a good omen. The sun is swallowed by the sky.

ONE BEACH

Sushi Nagato in Valencia. Now long internal orgasm. Across from banana split and space egg. Bus 19. 20 min to the beaches of Valencia. There is one beach with many names. The sun is burny. Mojitos y cerveza. Rapido y rapido. A warm wind from the sea. Pigs ears in my belly. It is easy to sink into this chair.

In the bathtub your pubic region becomes a strange sea creature. You sink the ship in the water. You dunk the yellow ducks. When you get out of the bath you are old and wrinkly. It is the greatest surprise. You are only temporary. A hazy green sea floats beneath you. Three fates stir the cauldron with twigs. Hybrid creatures. Egg shaped vessels with sacerdotal meat transit. Sugar skulls. Aztec marigolds and candied pumpkins. Bread of skull frosted with twisted bones. A dark dreambox of another kind.

SPACE DUST

During Day of the Dead November 2015 Chris is in Krakow eating pancakes. The sauce is very good he says. The pancakes are sweet scrolls of paper. The pancakes are fluffy pillows. The sauce of our days is sometimes sour. The sauce of our days is sometimes sweet. Parachutes of fire fall from the heavens. The yellow lemons drive out the devils. The great urn is full of space dust.

The local priest held a festival once a month for youthful vigour. He made everyone kiss the turtle in his box. One day the centipedes caught on. They invaded the big box full of the bones of youthful vigour. They lined up their centipede bodies and ate the priest. They made a new turtle. The new turtle was called William Butler Yeats.

THE MOUSE'S HOROSCOPE

for Max Ernst

I open Loplop and the Mouse's Horoscope. Long bony fingers measure the length of the mouse. The mouse runs from the door of one house to another. This is traced with dotted lines. The dotted lines form a half circle. It is the letter U. The man holds a black hat in his other hand. And also elegant clothing. Did he come from the opera. He is very bony. You can see all of his ribs. He is very hungry. It is civilisation without its clothes. It is the true measure of progress. The true ideas behind invisible things. A deeply romantic way of thinking.

The nuts are coated in curry. There is an orange dog in the corner. The floor is cold concrete. It is very authentic. Russian aristocratic ladies to my left. Spanish artistic fashionistas to my right. A man tries to steal a loaf of bread. He is brought back inside the shop by his ear. The young Russian aristocrats are chewing daintily on triangles of toast. The orange dog is wagging its tail. It paws the floor and chews the rest of the bread. The balconies are full of empty stone flower pots. French ladies talk in streams of smoke. I trace the lines on my hands. I extend my leg off the chair. I can still see the muscles in my quads. Very good. I point my toes in and raise myself twelve times. I point my toes out and raise myself twelve times. I point my toes straight and raise myself twelve times. I can still see the muscles in my calves. Very good. I shift my hat to the back part of my head.

We went inside and the heavy door closed behind us. Everything was glow red. How do we get out of here I asked. We don't they sed. We have to wait they sed. I better freshen up I sed. There is a small sink in the corner they sed. I pulled out a collapsible toothbrush from my back pocket and began scrubbing. I gurgled and spit. Watery blood lined the sink. Blood is a warning sign. Don't ignore it they sed. Stick out your tongue they sed. I stuck out my tongue halfway. Wider they sed. I have to see it all. Too much white foam on top and a bit grey in the back they sed. You have a hard time making up your mind but mostly you are too sweet they sed. I gurgled and gurgled but the white foam stayed on my tongue. Someone finally opened the door and let us out of the heart room. I went to market to buy knock off perfume. And then some wedgies. I woke up at 5AM after two hours sleep. My feet were clammy and my hands were clammy and my mouth was a dry cave. I found a small black box by my pillow. I opened the small box. It made a creaking sound. Inside was a small wooden stake. A miniature stake. I went back to the party. No one was there. There was only a dummy on the wooden porch. I staked the dummy. Right through the heart. All better I said. All better it sed.

I am not a manly man. The manly men wear studly belts. The beepers sit on their studly belts. The beepers buzz. It is a very strong buzz. It is very studly. I do not have a beeper. I am not a stud. I open the door to my Metro. My Metro runs on two small horses. It is also an electric insect. It buzzes around the mountain. It is not a studly Metro. She hands me a small round ball. It is a mouth grenade. It is a small round ball of raw meat. I look at my ball. Dora chews her ball. Come on she says. Chew your ball. I can see you are a wild man. Deep down she says. I open the door to my small red Metro. The Metro is an electric insect. It buzzes down the mountain. I step inside Dora's living room. There are three cacti pots on her glass table. I like cacti she says. Cacti are wild she says. I walk toward the cacti. They are prickly and manly. I pick them up one by one. Hordes of wee flying insects are buzzing around them. I squish one. Then ten. Then twenty. A hundred more come. We can't win I say. We can never win she says.

I stepped inside the wooden restaurant. A hurly burly man came to the dinner table. He was tall and also bearded. He took my girlfriend and they had their way with each other. I cannot grow any taller I said. But I can grow a beard. And thus began the beard growing. I have to shave my neck I said. It gets too itchy. Fair enough she said. I have to shave around my lips I said. I don't like hair in my mouth. Fair enough she said. Many years went by. My beard was very long. I must have won. I was inside a log cabin. The log cabin was in the hands of a small boy. I looked out of the log cabin. It was a jungle of carpet. It was so thick. It must have been the seventies. Disco hits were spinning somewhere in another room. And thus I began my journey with a plastic knife. I hacked my way through the carpet. It was very itchy. I reached the kitchen. My beard trailing along the ground. Where do I come from? Where am I going? Why am I here? The universe has an ancestor. Another universe. Born inside a black hole. The universe reproduces with black holes. No black holes means no reproduction. You need a black hole. Where is your black hole? Only survival of the fittest. Black holes. I must find my black hole I said. I climbed the cupboard and reached a very bulky microwave. I stepped inside. The radio waves whooshed. Ding. I woke up inside an 80's microwave. It was smaller. The radio waves whooshed. Ding. I woke up inside a millennium microwave. The microwaves were getting smaller. They were evolving. The big bang is now the big bounce. The universe is a wave. The universe is a string theory. An unexplained patch of nothing in cosmic microwave background radiation. I stepped back inside. I bounced around. I was a real human.

In Spanish if you are a good fit for a job you are a bug in the house he says. A bug in the house I ask. A bug in the house he says. I thought I might be a bug in the house he says. I ticked all the boxes but they already had a bug in the house he says. I open the window and a bug comes in the house. I squish it with my green lottery ticket. I must examine it I say. I lift the green lottery ticket to my eyes. My right eye is weaker. It is oblong. A deflated football. I put a spoon over my right eye and look at it with my left. It is small and light black. It has a little antenna for feeling its way in the world. Is it a baby I ask. Maybe he sighs. Is it a stink bug I ask. I hope we don't stink. Maybe he sighs. Is it a bed bug. I do not like to bed down with bed bugs. Maybe he sighs. Is it a mite. It might be a mite. Maybe he sighs. We lean closer. We need a microscope I say. We are not scientists he says. What is our job I say. We have no job he says. We buy another lottery ticket. We buy another lottery ticket. And also another. Up in the corner there is a small fly. It is a translucent eyeball. It is the eye of god.

We soaked our feet and hands in warm water. We washed the dishes for ten hours at Sizzler. Cigarette butts & egg yolks. Beans and lobsters. We wrinkled and wrinkled. We were old men. Or young babies. Hand me down jumpers. Hand me down trousers. Can you please close the window said Marek. We have to keep the window open I said. We need to toughen up I said. We rode our bikes up the steep hills. And also far outside of town. A healthy body is a healthy mind I said. We collapsed on our mattresses late in the evening. A bag of potatoes.

Just as the people playing the people who lived during the time of the red moon are leaving the tunnel and the butcher who plays the butcher is killed by the real butcher there is a loud pop in the kitchen. And then another and another. Yellow yolk drips down the wall. And also the clothesline. We shouldn't have left the window open says Nell. They begin scrubbing the wall with blue spray. They lean out of the window. They wipe the shutters. It is egg. They wipe down all the shelves. It is egg. They wipe the coffee pot. It is egg. They wipe the hob and the saucepan and the tea cups and saucers and cereal bowls. It is egg. They sit back down. The egg yolk has the most calories. Yeah says Noreen. You use egg whites for cake. I wish we had cake. You can't have cake on Halloween. You need candy says Nell. Like tiny wax corn candies. It is truly American. True says Noreen. We don't have any American candy. Is popcorn American? Popcorn is probably american says Nell. Just as the popcorn is popping there is another pop. And another and another. More eggs. They roll down the metal shutters. Time to seal the ark says Nell.

Jerry twiddles his gold chain. And his frosted fringe. He has a hard body. Biceps, chest, back muscles. Also his hair is hard. It is full of hairspray. He leans over the bread and dangles his gold chain. There is nothing on his gold chain. It is just a gold chain. On gym days you can see his cleavage. He reads the prayer for the body. I read the prayer for the blood. After all the singing we walk to the back room. Should we make the wads he asks. Sure I say. To make a good wad you roll four or five pieces of Jesus body together. Jesus body is Wonder Bread. It always tastes different than the regular body. All the hand rolling adds extra salt says Jerry. Stick the wad in your gums says Jerry. We stick the wads in our gums. We make it juicy. Leftovers always taste better says Jerry.

To be a good student of milk you need to know the subject. If you know the subject you know the milk. This is called saber la leche. Darse una leche means to give oneself a milk. I bumped into the door. I gave myself a milk today. To be in a bad mood is mala leche. It is Monday morning and I am mala leche. I am bad milk. In English we say to be the shit but in Spanish they say to be the milk. Ser la leche is to be the milk. This is very good. Me cago en la leche means I crap in the milk. I crapped the milk this morning. It was very old. I did not smell it. This is very bad. Just before siesta the crowds in the metro are at full milk. This is called toda leche. You have to use your elbows. The cars before siesta are conducir a toda leche. They drive very fast. On Fridays the neighbours thump their music to get ready for the weekend. They tenía la música a toda leche. You have to be careful about spilling the milk. Vehicles driving at full milk with the radio blaring at full milk are very likely to end up using another milk. This is called darse una leche. If you have good fortune you have good milk. Milk is tremendous. It is una suerte de la leche. To be really smart is la leche de listo. I am learning the milk.

STRAIGHT TALK

The deer are twitching their tails at Deer Park. They won't stop twitching. It is the heated season. They scrape their antlers. Run two by two. Then they all sit down in a clearing for dinner. Everything cools and stretches then life pops out. This is called the universe. Earthlings we are many. Separation equals extinction. Nature is squiggly. Words are straight. How can they get along?

I'm afraid of getting my soul sucked. I've had my soul sucked. Have you had your soul sucked? Where did you get your soul sucked? Who sucked your soul and why did they suck your soul? Soul sucking is voluntary. And sometimes involuntary. How many souls have you sucked? How many people have sucked your soul? When will you stop sucking souls? Do you want to stop sucking souls? When did you first start sucking souls? Do you prefer sucking souls or having your soul sucked? If soul sucking stopped tomorrow what would you suck? Would you stop sucking? What was your favourite soul suck? What is your average soul suck? How many soul sucks do you prefer per day? How many souls can you suck at one time? When you suck a soul how do you feel before and after? When you have your soul sucked do you think of sucking someone else's soul? What do you think about when sucking a soul or having your soul sucked?

SMUDGE

I am an ancient Irish monk. In a cave. Bent over ancient books copying copying copying. & the waves are crashing on sharp rocks below me. This is all very romantic but I am in a lab. Full of the light of scientific reasoning. The light overhead on the ceiling is shining on my iPad. This is called glare. When the light is glaring at you you have to squint. You become myopic. When my iPad turns off it is smudged. There are traces of many fingerprints. Our fingers are getting faster and faster. This is the evolution of Homo Sapiens. What a strange creature. Soon we will go into the machine. The machine will ask different questions. I don't know what kind of questions. This poem is for the machines.

HOLY GHOST

The holy ghost says count to ten. The holy ghost says count to twenty. The holy ghost says count to thirty. Very good says the holy ghost. I am waiting for my bosom to burn. The holy ghost burns the bosom. The holy ghost tells me everything. I have to listen very carefully. The holy ghost says don't step on that crack. Step on the other one. The holy ghost says don't step on that crack. Step on the other one. Very good says the holy ghost. The holy ghost says wash your hands. The holy ghost says wash your hands. The holy ghost says wash your hands. Very good says the holy ghost. The holy ghost is coming. The holy ghost is not coming. I look in the mirror. Goodbye holy ghost.

FEEDBACK

for Will May

I like that antique tea wagon and small television. I like the computer built by your brother. I like the man in the yellow jacket as the guide. I like free-will and predestination and fate. I like how the mind reaches out to touch, literally, the light of the stars. I like how the reader is possessed. I like illusions of self that each new self is born into. I like if you love someone set them on fire. I like how the older lady steals the parking space. I like the sickness of soul. I like how the reader is also being watched by the narrator. The kangaroo leather documentary in the pub really pulled me in. The many levels of watching really pulled me in. I like how the narrator flickers in and out. The last chapter is sharp and honest. The last chapter has many serpents eating their tails. This builds habits of nature. This builds emotional connection. This embodies the novel.

ACKNOWLEDGEMENTS

Special thanks to the editors of the following journals for publishing some of the poems in *The Green Monk* (sometimes in different forms):

Bear Review, Tin House, *Poetry*, *Poems in Which*, *For Every Year*, *Likewise Folio*, *Poets and Artists, Daily Gramma, Fluland, The Elephants, Reality Beach, Stockholm Review of Literature, The Moth.*

'The Underground' was chosen for *Best British Poetry 2015*. Thank you, Emily Berry.

As always, special thanks to Ewa Rasała for her editorial guidance, loving support, and amazing mind.

The Green Monk
By Marcus Slease

First published in this edition by Boiler House Press, 2018
Part of UEA Publishing Project

Design and typesetting by Emily Benton
emilybentonbookdesigner.co.uk

Typeset in Arnhem
Printed by Imprint Digital, UK
Distributed by NBN International

ISBN 978-1-911343-48-6